Contents

Welcome 2

(1) Free time 8

(2) Wild animals 18

(3) The seasons 28

(4) My week 38

(5) Jobs 48

(6) In the rainforest 58

(7) Feelings 68

(8) Action! 78

Goodbye 88

Festivals 92

Review 96

Picture dictionary 104

T0385997

1 Write and match.

1 She's 9. She's got black hair.

She likes pink. Her name's

_____Ruby_____.

2 She's 11. She's got red hair.

She likes films. Her name's

_____.

3 He's 8. He's got blond hair.

He likes skateboards. His name's

_____.

4 He's 8. He's got red hair.

He's got a sister. His name's

_____.

2 Draw or stick a picture of yourself and a friend. Then write.

My name's _____.

I am _____ years old.

I like _____.

My friend's name is _____.

_____ is _____ years old.

_____ likes _____.

Lesson 1 grammar (introductions and greetings)

3 Write.

1 My name's Ruby. I've got a pink skirt and a pink blouse. _____I've got_____ glasses and white trainers.

2 My name's Sam. _____ a red hat, green _____, a white shirt and black and white trainers.

3 I'm John. _____ a black T-shirt, brown trousers and black _____.

4 I'm Jenny. _____ purple trousers, a pink T-shirt and _____ trainers.

4 Write about yourself and your partner.

My name's _____. I've got _____ and _____.

My partner's name is _____. He's/She's got _____ and _____.

5 🔘 1:05 **Listen and match.**

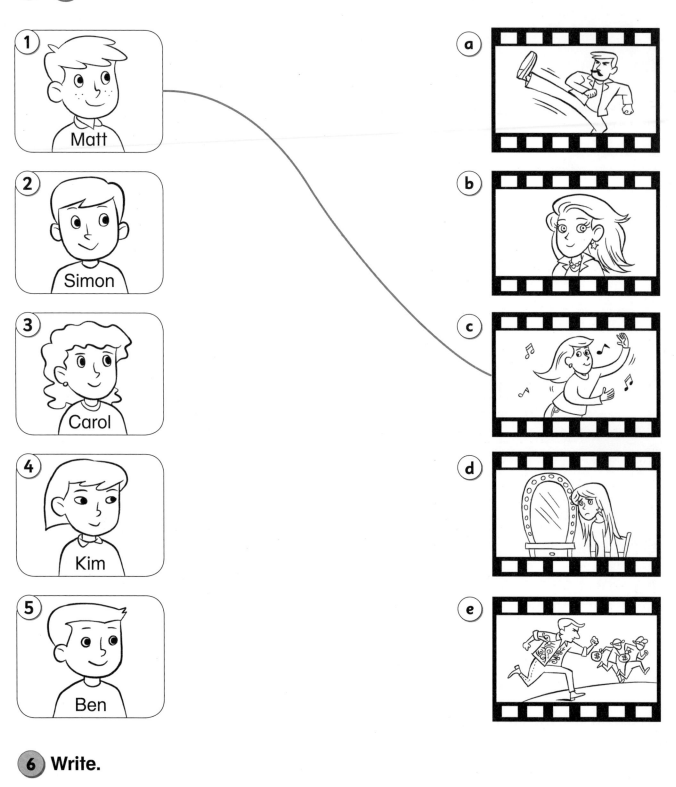

1 Matt

2 Simon

3 Carol

4 Kim

5 Ben

a

b

c

d

e

6 **Write.**

My favourite film star is _____. _____ can

_____ .

7  **Listen and write the numbers.**

a 84				

b				

c				

d				

8 **Write.**

50	60	70
fifty		

80	90	100

9 **Write your favourite numbers.**

1   My favourite number between 1 and 10 is _____.

2   My favourite number between 10 and 50 is _____.

3   My favourite number between 50 and 100 is _____.

10 **Look and circle.**

1 A horse is (shorter /(taller)) than a mouse.

2 A mouse is (bigger / smaller) than a cat.

3 A rabbit is (faster / slower) than a tortoise.

4 A cat is (smaller / bigger) than a dog.

5 A dog is (shorter / taller) than a horse.

11 **Look and write.**

Billy
12 years old

Andy
7 years old

Sue
9 years old

Darren
11 years old

Jane
10 years old

Christine
8 years old

1 (old / young)   Billy is _____ older than _____ Andy.

2 (old / young)   Darren is _____ Billy.

3 (clever / young) Sue is _____ Christine.

4 (clever / young) Jane is _____ Darren.

12 Read and draw.

1

He's taller than me.

2

Her hands are bigger than his.

3

A mouse is smaller than a cat.

4

A rabbit is smaller than a dog.

1 Free time

1 Match.

chatting online

watching TV

reading the newspaper

skiing

playing the guitar

playing computer games

cooking

skateboarding

2 Look and write.

1 He doesn't like __playing computer games__.

2 He likes _____.

3 He _____.

4 He _____.

3 🔘 1:16 **Listen and write ✓ = likes or ✗ = doesn't like.**

4 **Look at Activity 3 and write.**

1 What does Ruby like doing?

She likes _____skiing_____ and _____.

She doesn't like _____ or _____.

2 What does John like doing?

He likes _____ and _____.

He doesn't like _____ or _____.

5 **Write.**

What do you like doing?

I like _____.

I don't like _____.

6 🔊 1:19 **Listen and write Y = Yes or N = No.**

1 Y

2

3

4

7 **Look at Activity 6 and write.**

> painting   playing hockey   riding a scooter   walking the dog

1 Does she like _____ playing hockey _____ ? _____ Yes _____ , she _____ does _____ .

2 Does he like _____ ? _____ , he _____ .

3 Do they like _____ ? _____ , they _____ .

4 Does he like _____ ? _____ , he _____ .

8 **Write.**

1 Do you like _____ skipping _____ ? _____ , I _____ .

2 Do you like _____ ?

3 Do you like _____ ?

4 Do you like _____ ?

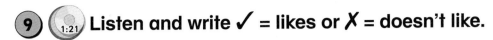

9 (1:21) **Listen and write ✓ = likes or ✗ = doesn't like.**

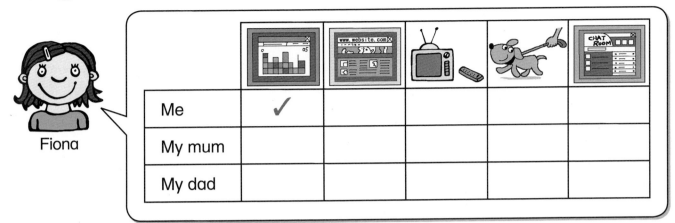

Me	✓				
My mum					
My dad					

Fiona

10 Look at Activity 9 and write.

1 Does Fiona like playing computer games? ____Yes, she does.____

2 Does Fiona like watching TV? _____

3 What does Fiona's mum like doing? She likes _____.

She also likes _____ and _____.

4 What does Fiona's dad like doing? He likes _____.

He also likes _____ and _____.

11 Write questions and answers.

1  Does _____

_____

2  _____

_____

11

Lesson 4 grammar *(Do you like skipping? Yes, I do. / No, I don't.)*

12 **Read the story again. What does Cleo like doing? Write.**

_____

13 **Number the pictures in order.**

14 **Write.**

| eating   listening   looking   lying |
| sleeping   watching |

1 Ruby, John, Jenny and Sam are ____looking____ for Madley Kool.

2 The man in the studio says that Cleo likes _____ and

_____.

3 Cleo likes _____ in the sun.

4 Cleo likes _____ and looking and _____.

15 Read the words. Circle the pictures.

blow   cloud   shout   snow

16 (1:26) Listen and connect the letters. Then write.

1   b   ear   _____

2   ch   ay   _____

3   d   oy   _____boy_____

4   y   air   _____

17 (1:27) Listen and write the words.

1 ____out____   2 _____   3 _____   4 _____

18 (1:28) Read aloud. Then listen and check.

It's wintertime. The wind blows and black clouds are low. There is a lot of snow. Wear a coat, a hat and a scarf when you go out.

19 **Listen and read. Then write.**

This is Megan. She lives in a special house. It's a castle. It's got 21 rooms and a big garden. She likes playing in the garden and reading outside. In the morning she can hear the swans but at night it's very quiet. She doesn't like cleaning the castle, it's too big!

Name	Megan
House	
Description	
Animals	
Likes	
Doesn't like	

20 **Listen and tick (✓).**

1

2

21 **Draw or stick a photo of a special house.**

Wider World

**22 Read and write
T = True or F = False.**

① Kelly's blog

Hi, I'm Kelly. I'm from Canada. It's snowy here in winter. I like skiing. It's fun. I can go very fast and jump very high! Do you like skiing?

Kelly, 9, Canada

② Tumelo's blog

Hi, I'm Tumelo. I'm from South Africa. I like playing football at school with my friends. I can see the Soccer City stadium from my house. It's really big. My favourite team is the Mamelodi Sundowns.

Tumelo, 9, South Africa

1 Kelly likes skiing. | T |

2 Kelly can't ski fast. | |

3 Kelly can jump very high. | |

4 Tumelo likes playing football at school. | |

5 The stadium is not very big. | |

6 His favourite football team is the Mamelodi Sundowns. | |

Unit Review

23 Look and write.

Across →

Down ↓

1. w a l k i n g

24 Look and write.

playing computer games ✓
reading the newspaper ✓
playing the guitar ✗

skiing ✓
riding a scooter ✗
watching TV ✓

1   What does she like doing? She likes ____playing computer games____

and _____.

2   _____? No, she doesn't.

3   What does he like doing? _____

4   He doesn't _____.

About Me

25 **What do or don't you like doing? Write ✓ or ✗.**

26 **Look at Activity 25 and write.**

I like _____

_____ .

I don't like _____

_____ .

27 **Write about your friends or family.**

1   My _____ likes _____ .

_____ doesn't like _____ .

2   My _____ .

_____ .

   I can say what I like or don't like doing. ☐

I can set goals for myself. ☐

2 Wild animals

1 🔘 1:37 **Listen and number.**

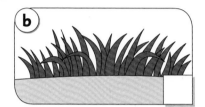

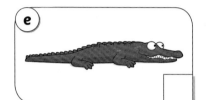

2 **Look and write.**

crocodile   elephant   hippo   giraffe   lion   monkey

It's a lion. _____   _____

_____   _____   _____

3 **What do the animals eat? Write.**

fruit   grass   leaves   meat

1 _____Monkeys eat fruit._____   2 _____

3 _____   4 _____

5 _____   6 _____

4 **Look and write.**

	Fruit	Leaves	Grass	Insects	Meat
Monkeys	✓	✗	✗	✓	✓
Lions	✗	✗	✗	✗	✓
Elephants	✓	✓	✓	✗	✗
Crocodiles	✗	✗	✗	✓	✓

1 Do monkeys eat fruit? _____Yes, they do._____

2 Do lions eat insects? _____

3 _____ elephants _____ fruit? _____

4 _____ crocodiles _____? _____

5 _____   _____

5 Match.

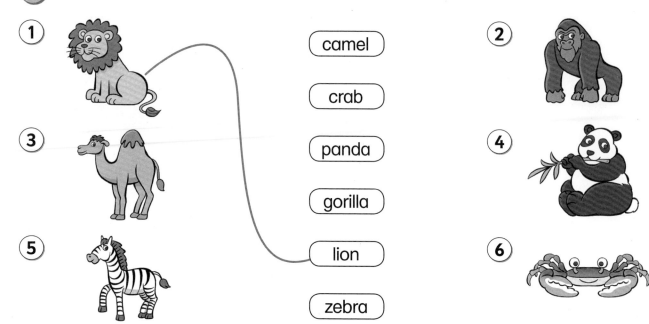

1. [lion]
2. [gorilla]
3. [camel]
4. [panda]
5. [zebra]
6. [crab]

camel

crab

panda

gorilla

lion

zebra

6 Unscramble and write. Then number.

1 oferts ➡ _____forest_____

2 tesedr ➡ _____

3 lsgasrand ➡ _____

4 rernfoista ➡ _____

5 evrir ➡ _____

a 1
b
c
d
e

7 (1:42) Listen and write.

1 _____Zebras_____ live in _____.

2 _____ live in _____.

3 _____ live in _____.

Lesson 3 vocabulary / grammar (wild animals / habitats)

8 **Look and write.**

playing   fast   slowly

1 _____Camels_____ eat grass. They drink very little water. They can run fast but

they walk _____. They can walk all day.

2 _____ eat bamboo, leaves and insects. They like _____

with their friends. They can eat 38 kilos of food every day.

3 _____ eat a lot of grass and leaves. They drink water from rivers.

They run very _____. They've got black and white stripes.

9 **Look at Activity 8 and write.**

1 What do camels eat? They eat _____grass_____.

How much water do they drink? _____

Can they run fast? _____

2 What do _____? They eat _____.

How many kilos of food can they eat? _____

Do they like playing with their friends? _____

3 What do _____? They eat _____.

How much grass do they eat? _____

Can they run fast? _____

10 Read the story again. Do elephants eat cats? Write.

_____

11 Number the pictures in order.

Oh, they eat grass …

And where are the crocodiles?

Where are the hippos?

What do elephants eat?

1

12 Write.

1 Are elephants big? _____ Yes, they are. _____

2 What do elephants eat? _____

3 Who can't see the hippos or the crocodiles? _____

4 Where are the crocodiles? _____ John's _____.

5 Who rescues John? _____

13 Where do the animals live? Write.

forests   grasslands   rivers

1 Elephants live in ____ grasslands ____ and _____.

2 _____

3 _____

14 **Read the words. Circle the pictures.**

claw   draw   wall   yawn

15 (1:49) **Listen and connect the letters. Then write.**

1   th   i   n   er   _____

2   d   a   b   er   _____

3   s   u   nn   k   _thank_____

4   c   ow   mm   oy   _____

16 (1:50) **Listen and write the words.**

1   ___all___   2   _____   3   _____   4   _____

17 (1:51) **Read aloud. Then listen and check.**

Welcome to the zoo. Look at the big cats! They've got sharp teeth and sharp claws. I'm glad the wall is tall. You cats can't eat me for dinner!

18 **Read and write.**

Kinds of animals		
Herbivores (eat plants)	**Carnivores** (eat other animals)	**Omnivores** (eat plants and animals)
horses	dogs	bears
rabbits	cats	monkeys
elephants	lions	pigs
cows	tigers	mice
	snakes	

1 _____Herbivores_____ are animals that eat _____plants_____. Some herbivores

are horses, _____, _____ and cows.

2 _____ are animals that eat _____. Some carnivores

are dogs, cats, lions, _____ and _____.

3 _____ are animals that eat both _____ and

_____. Some omnivores are bears, monkeys, _____

and _____.

19 **Look at the food chain. Write.**

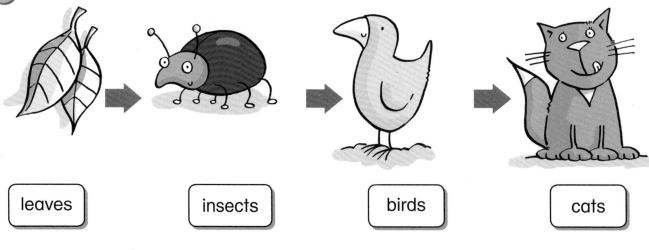

| leaves | insects | birds | cats |

Insects eat _____leaves_____, birds eat _____ and cats eat

_____.

Wider World

20 **Read and answer.**

I'm Akeyo. I live in the Serengeti National Park in Tanzania. The sun shines most days here and it's very hot. There are a lot of different animals in the park. I like the giraffes. They're tall and they've got long necks. They eat the leaves at the top of the trees.

Akeyo, 10, Tanzania

1 Where does Akeyo live?

She lives in the _____ Serengeti National Park in Tanzania.

2 Are there many different animals in the park? _____

3 What animals does she like? She likes _____.

4 What do they look like? They're _____ and they've got

_____.

5 What do they eat? _____

Unit Review

21 Write the animals' names. Then match.

1 2 3 4 5

gorilla _____ _____ _____ _____

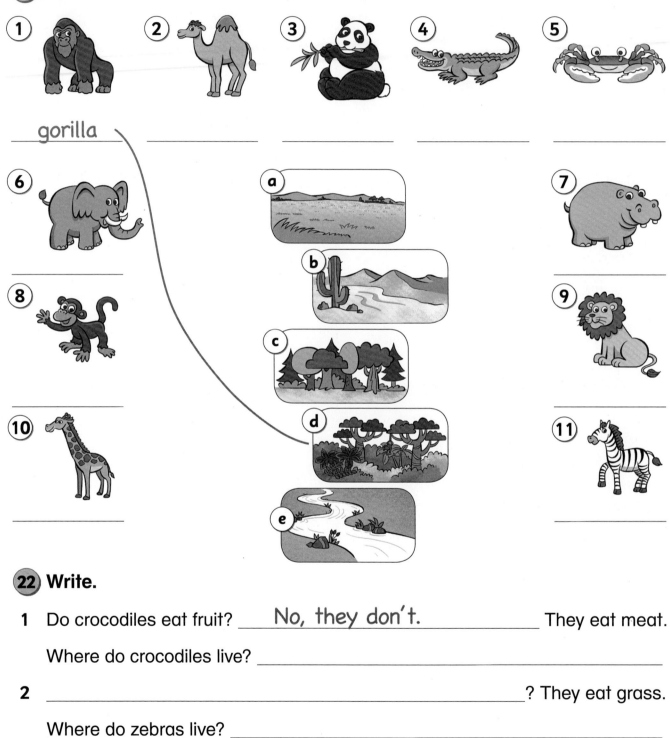

6

a

b

7

c

8

9

d

10

e

11

22 Write.

1 Do crocodiles eat fruit? _____No, they don't._____ They eat meat.

Where do crocodiles live? _____

2 _____? They eat grass.

Where do zebras live? _____

About Me

23 Draw or stick a photo of an animal. Then write.

Grassland	River
_____ live in _____.	_____ live in _____.
They eat _____.	They eat _____.
They can _____.	They can _____.
They can't _____.	They can't _____.
They walk _____.	They swim _____.

Desert	Near my town
_____	_____
_____	_____
_____	_____
_____	_____
_____	_____

 I can talk about animals, their food and where they live. ☐
I can help protect wild animals. ☐

3 The seasons

1 Match.

humid

lightning

stormy

thunder

warm

wet

2 Look at Activity 1 and write.

Hello, everybody. What's the weather like today? Here in the

north, it's ¹_____warm_____. The temperature is ²_____

degrees. Don't forget your hat!

Let's look at the east now. It's ³_____ today. The

temperature is ⁴_____.

Now, let's see the west. It's ⁵_____ today. It's cool.

The temperature is ⁶_____.

In the south the weather is ⁷_____. There's ⁸_____

and ⁹_____. It's ¹⁰_____.

3 🔘 1:60 **Listen and number.**

a  ☐

b 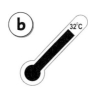 ☐

c  1

d  ☐

e 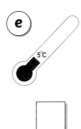 ☐

f  ☐

4 **Look and write.**

1 What's the weather like today?

There's ___thunder___ and

___lightning___.

2 What's the weather like today?

It's _____.

3 What's the weather like today?

It's _____.

4 What's the weather like today?

It's _____.

5 What's the temperature today?

It's _____.

6 What's the temperature today?

It's _____.

5 **Look and write.**

| autumn   spring   summer   winter |

1  **2**  **3**  **4**

It's ___autumn___ .   It's _____ .   It's _____ .   It's _____ .

6 **Look and write.**

| go camping   go hiking   go snowboarding   go water skiing |

1    **2**

___go snowboarding___   _____

3    **4**

_____   _____

7 **Look at Activity 6 and write.**

1 He ___goes snowboarding___ in ___winter___ .

2 She _____ in _____ .

3 He _____ in _____ .

4 They _____ in _____ .

8 **Read and number.**

1 She likes eating peaches in summer.

2 She goes to the park in winter.

3 She likes smelling the flowers in spring.

4 She likes flying her kite in autumn.

9 **Write.**

Look at this picture. This is me at the beach last summer. It was warm. I love going water skiing in summer.

I like this picture. It's me skiing last winter. It was cold at the ski slope. I love skiing in winter.

1 What was the weather like last summer?

_____It was warm._____

2 What was the temperature?

_____

3 What does she do in summer?

_____

4 What was the weather like last winter?

_____

5 What was the temperature?

_____

6 What does he do in winter?

_____

10 Read the story again. Why do they like the beach? Write.

_____

11 Look and write. Then number the pictures in order.

> Action!   I can sleep!   It's hot.
> It's wet!   There's a beach!   We can climb.

Action!
_____

_____

12 Look at Activity 11 and write.

a Is he a detective?   No, he isn't.
                    _____

b What can Sam do?   _____

c Where are they?   _____

d Is it snowy?   _____

e Is it rainy?   _____

13 **Read the words. Circle the pictures.**

| chew   fly   new   sky |

ew   y

14 (1:69) **Listen and connect the letters. Then write.**

1	l	oi	k	_____
2	c	ea	l	_____
3	m	ee	f	_leaf_
4	w	ai	n	_____

15 (1:70) **Listen and write the words.**

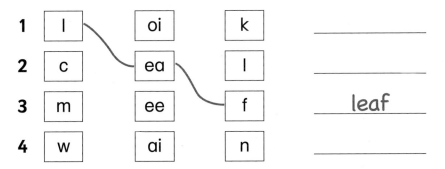

1 _stew_   2 _____   3 _____   4 _____

16 (1:71) **Read aloud. Then listen and check.**

In my new jet I fly up and down, high and low. I see the clouds and the sun, the rain and the snow. I like to be up in the sky.

17 Read and circle.

HURRICANE QUIZ

1 The centre of the hurricane is
A the heart.   B the eye.

2 In the centre of the hurricane
A it's windy.   B it isn't windy.

3 There are hurricanes in the
A summer and autumn.
B winter and spring.

18 Write *hurricane*, *typhoon* or *cyclone*.

Korea

typhoon

the United States

_____

Australia

_____

China

_____

Wider World

19 **Read and match.**

1

tornado

earthquake

big waves

strong storm

one thousand a year

Japan

Texas

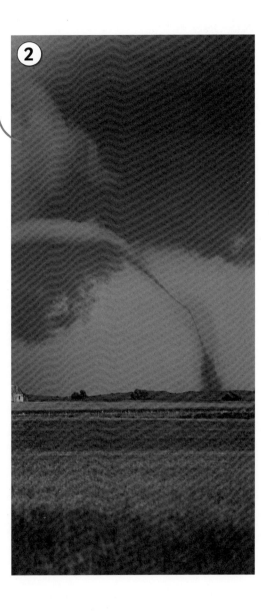

2

20 **Answer.**

1   Are there earthquakes in your country? _____

2   Are there tsunamis in your country? _____

3   Are there tornadoes in your country? _____

4   Do you build strong buildings in your country? _____

Unit Review

21 Look and write.

Across ➡

1 It's rainy. It's [image].

3 It's hot and [image].

5 The ____ today is 18°.

7 18° means 18 ____.

Down ⬇

2 I can hear KA-BOOM! .

4 I can see [image].

6 It's [image]. Let's go to the beach.

8 It's [image]. We can't go to the beach.

```
       ¹w  e  ²t
               ³□ □ □ □ □
  ⁴□        
  □      ⁶□          ⁸□
  □      □          □
 ⁵□ □ □ □ □ □ □ □ □ □ □
  □      □          □
  □     ⁷□ □ □ □ □ □ □
  □                □
```

22 Write.

> goes camping   go snowboarding   go water skiing
> spring   summer   winter

Hi. It's ¹____winter____ here and it's really cold. I ²_____

and skiing with my friends. I don't like spring because it's rainy but my sister

loves it. She ³_____ in ⁴_____. What's your

favourite season?

Hi. It's ⁵_____ here and it's warm. I love the beach.

I ⁶_____ in summer when the water is warm. It's my

favourite season. I don't really like autumn because it's windy.

23 Think and write.

What was the weather like yesterday? It _____.

About Me

24 Draw or stick a picture of your favourite season.

25 Write an email to your friend about your favourite season.

Hi, _____. It's _____ here and it's _____.

_____

_____

_____

_____

_____

_____

I CAN

I can describe the weather and the seasons. ☐

I can say what I like doing during the different seasons. ☐

4 My week

1 Match.

do karate

do gymnastics

have ballet lessons

have music lessons

learn to cook

learn to draw

practise the piano

practise the violin

study English

study Maths

2 Write.

What do you do on Saturdays?

do   have   learn to
practise   study

1 I _____do_____ gymnastics.

2 I _____ music lessons.

3 I _____ the piano.

4 I _____ karate.

5 I _____ the violin.

6 I _____ ballet lessons.

7 I _____ Maths.

8 I _____ cook.

9 I _____ English.

10 I _____ draw.

3 Look and write.

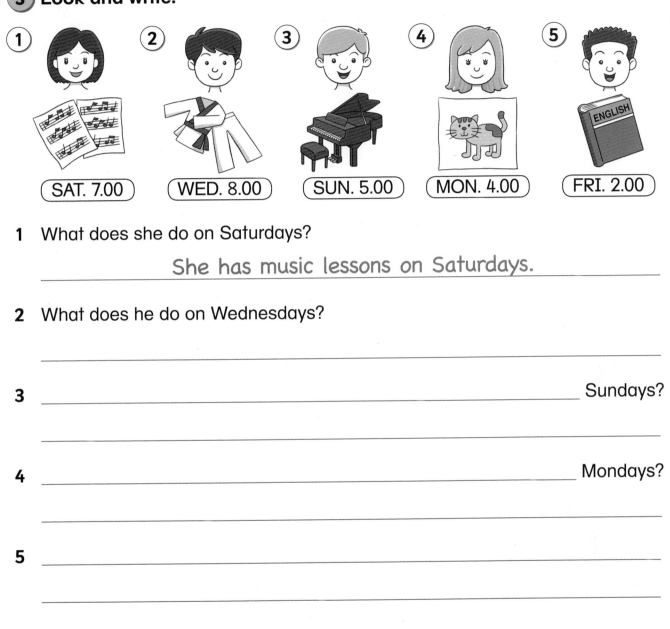

(1) SAT. 7.00
(2) WED. 8.00
(3) SUN. 5.00
(4) MON. 4.00
(5) FRI. 2.00

1 What does she do on Saturdays?

She has music lessons on Saturdays.

2 What does he do on Wednesdays?

_____

3 _____ Sundays?

_____

4 _____ Mondays?

_____

5 _____

_____

4 Look at Activity 3 and write.

1 She has music lessons at 7 o'clock.

2 _____

3 _____

4 _____

5 _____

Lesson 2 grammar (*What do you do on Saturdays? I practise the piano on Saturdays.*)

5 Look and write.

afternoon   a quarter past 8   a quarter to 9   evening
half past 3   midday   morning

 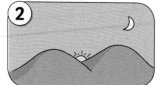  

morning   _____   _____   _____

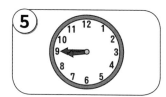 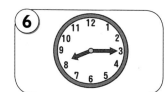 

_____   _____   _____

6 Listen and match.

7 (2:10) **Listen and draw the time. Then write.**

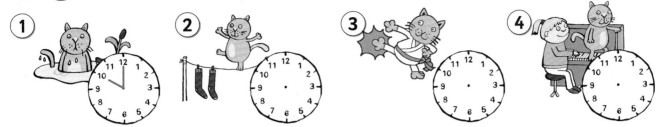

1 She goes swimming at _____10 o'clock_____.

2 She _____ at _____.

3 She _____ at _____.

4 _____

8 **Look and write.**

When does she learn to cook?

She learns to cook _in the morning._

When does he _____?

_____

_____ ?

_____

_____ ?

_____

9 **Write about you.**

1 _I always_ _____ (always)

2 _____ (often)

3 _____ (never)

10 Read the story again. Can Madley sing and do karate? Write.

_____

11 Number the pictures in order.

On Saturdays …

On Fridays …

but he can't swim!

Where is Madley?

1

On Mondays …

12 Look at Activity 11 and write.

1   What does Madley Kool do on Mondays? <u>On Mondays he does karate.</u>

2   When does he have singing lessons? _____

_____

3   When does he go swimming? _____

4   Can he swim? _____

13 Write.

1   Does Madley walk to work?

_____

2   Has he got a car?

_____ He goes

_____ by _____ .

14 Read the words. Circle the pictures.

glue lie pie tie

ie   ue

15 🔊 2:15 Listen and connect the letters. Then write.

1	c	i	ke	_cake_
2	h	a	pe	_____
3	d	a	me	_____
4	sh	o	ve	_____

16 🔊 2:16 Listen and write the words.

1 _fried_   2 _____   3 _____   4 _____

17 🔊 2:17 Read aloud. Then listen and check.

Ha-ha-ha! The man with the tie has got glue on his boots. He can't run. He is stuck with the pie in his hand.

18 (2:20) **Listen and write. Then number.**

① I ___walk___ to school.
Alex

② Meiling
I go to school by _____.

③ I go to school by _____.
Jodie

④ Kabir
I go to school by _____.

a

b

c   1

d

19 **How do you and your friends go to school? Tick (✓) and write.**

	By car	By bus	By bike	By boat	By train	Walk
1 Me						
2						
3						

1   I _____.

2   _____ goes _____.

3   _____

Wider World

20 **Read and write.**

on Sundays
toys
the bus
cinemas
there are

In many cities ¹ ___there are___ shopping centres. Many shopping centres open 12 hours every day. They are open on Saturdays and even ² _____. There you can buy food, drinks, ³ _____, games and more. There are often restaurants, ⁴ _____, cafés and many shops. Shopping centres are usually in the town centre. Most people drive or take ⁵ _____ to get there.

21 **Look at Activity 20 and answer.**

1   How many hours do many shopping centres open?
     ___12 hours___

2   Do they open on Saturdays?
     _____

3   What can you buy there?
     _____

4   Are there restaurants in shopping centres?
     _____

5   Are shopping centres in the town centre?
     _____

Unit Review

22 (2:22) **Listen, number and tick (✓).**

 a

 b

1  a

 b ✓

 a

 b

 a

 b

23 What does Julie do on Saturdays? Write.

Julie's schedule	
8.00 – 9.00	4÷2= 8÷4= 2×2= 3×7=
9.15 – 10.00	(music notes)
11.00 – 12.00	(ballet shoes)
1.30 – 2.00	(piano)
2.45 – 3.30	(bench)
4.00 – 4.30	(cooking pot)

She studies Maths at 8 o'clock.

About Me

24 **Write one activity and time for each day.**

SUN	MON	TUES	WED
Study Maths, afternoon			

THURS	FRI	SAT

25 **Look at Activity 24. Write your own questions and answers.**

1 What do you do on Sundays? _____

On Sundays I always study Maths in the afternoon. _____

2 _____

On Wednesdays _____.

3 _____

On Fridays _____.

4 _____

On Saturdays _____.

5 _____

On Tuesdays _____.

6 _____

On Thursdays _____.

 I can talk about my daily activities. ☐

I can do surveys. ☐

5 Jobs

1 Look and write.

| a e i o u |

1 f <u>i r e</u> f <u>i</u> gh t <u>e</u> r

2 b__sk__tb__ll pl__y__r

3 b__ll__t d__nc__r

4 p__l__c__ __ff__c__r

5 b____ld__r

6 f__lm st__r

7 __str__n____t

2 Look and write.

2 I'm a
_____.

1 I'm an
astronaut
_____.

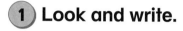

3 I'm a
_____.

4 I'm a
_____.

5 I'm a
_____.

3 Listen and number.

a ☐   b ☐   c 1   d ☐

e ☐   f ☐   g ☐

4 Look at Activity 3 and write.

1 What does she want to be? <u>She wants to be a police officer.</u>

 2 What does he want to be? _____

3 _____ does _____ want to be?

_____

 4 What does _____?

_____

5 _____ want to be?

_____

 6 _____?

_____

7 _____?

_____

5 **Look and write.**

athlete   carpenter   journalist   lawyer   mechanic
model   photographer   singer

1 _journalist_   2 _____   3 _____   4 _____

5 _____   6 _____   7 _____   8 _____

6 **Unscramble and write.**

1 he / want / does / to / a / be /
model (✗)

Does he want to be a

model?

No, he doesn't.

2 want / be / to / lawyer / does / a /
she (✔)

_____

_____

_____

3 a / do / want / be / to / you /
photographer (✔)

_____

_____

4 singer / he / want / does / to / a /
be (✗)

_____

_____

7 (2:33) **Listen and tick (✓) or cross (✗).**

1 **a** ✓   **b** ✗

2 **a** COURT   **b**

3 **a**   **b**

4 **a**   **b** POLICE

8 (2:34) **Listen again. Then write.**

1 He wants to be a ___journalist___ because he wants to _____.

He doesn't want to be a _____.

2 She _____.

She _____.

3 Why does she want to be _____?

She _____ because _____.

4 Why _____?

He _____.

9 **Write the questions. Then write your own answers.**

1 Do you _____? _____, I _____.

2 _____

_____

3 _____

_____

10 Read the story again. Why does John want to be a film star? Write.

_____

11 Look and write.

| acting   animals   dancing   jumping |

①

She loves _____dancing_____.

She wants to be a _____

_____.

②

_____

_____

_____

③

_____

_____

_____

④

_____

_____

_____

12 What do you want to be? Write.

13 **Read the words. Circle the pictures.**

jungle   paddle   rainy   sunny

le   y

14 (2:39) **Listen and connect the letters. Then write.**

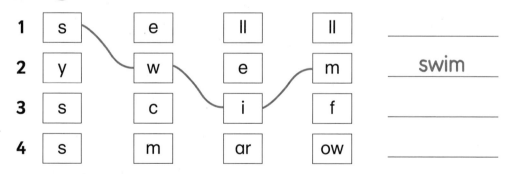

1 | s | e | ll | ll | _____
2 | y | w | e | m | swim
3 | s | c | i | f | _____
4 | s | m | ar | ow | _____

15 (2:40) **Listen and write the words.**

1 ___little___   2 _____   3 _____   4 _____

16 (2:41) **Read aloud. Then listen and check.**

We paddle down the river in our boat. The jungle is loud and the sun is hot. Look at that yellow snake! Look at that red and blue bird!

17 (2:44) **Listen and circle.**

1

Hello, Matthew. What do you want to be and why?

I want to be a (⚽ / 🏀) player because I love sports.

2

What do you do to make your dreams come true?

I go running at (🕘 / 🕕) in the morning. I eat only healthy food like (🍎🥗 / 🍫🍬). In the afternoon I practise (🏃 / 🤾) with the team.

3

What other things do you do?

I (🤸 / 🏊) on Sundays. I want to make my body strong.

18 **Draw your dream job. Then write.**

I want to be _____

because I _____

_____ .

_____

_____

Wider World

19 **Read and write.**

Lionel Messi

Santiago's blog

I'm Santiago. I'm from Argentina. I like playing football. I want to be a famous football player one day. My favourite team is Boca Juniors. There are a lot of good football players from Argentina. My favourite is Lionel Messi. He can run very fast and he scores a lot of goals.

Santiago, 10, Argentina

Kate's blog

Hello! I'm Kate. I'm from Ireland. I like watching films. I have singing and dancing lessons at school. I want to be a film star. My favourite film star is Emma Watson. She's very pretty and she's a good actor.

Kate, 9, Ireland

Emma Watson

1 Who wants to be a film star? _____

2 Who wants to be a football player? _____

20 **Read and write T = True or F = False.**

1 Kate likes watching films. ☐ T

2 Santiago hasn't got a favourite football team. ☐

3 Emma Watson is an actor. ☐

4 Lionel Messi is a basketball player. ☐

Unit Review

21 Look and write the jobs.

1   _police officer_   2   _____

3   _____   4   _____

5  _____   6   _____

7   _____   8  _____

22 Listen, number and tick (✓). Then write.

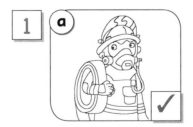

1 _____Does he want to be a firefighter?_____ Yes, he does.

2 _____ No, she doesn't.

3 What does she want to be? _____

4 What does he want to be? _____

About Me

23 Draw and write two things you want to be and two things you don't want to be.

✓

I want to be _____

because _____

_____ .

_____

_____

_____

✗

I don't want to be _____ .

_____

 I can talk about what I want to be.

I can plan for the future.

6 In the rainforest

1 Match.

(bridge) (hut) (mountain) (nest) (valley) (vines) (waterfall)

2 Look and write.

| across between and near over |

1 2 3 4

1 I'm swimming _____across_____ the _____river_____.

2 The bird is flying _____ the _____.

3 She's standing _____ the _____.

4 The _____ is _____ the lake _____ the trees.

3 Look and write.

 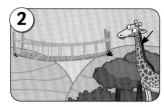  

1 Where's the doctor? She's _____near the vines_____ .

2 _____ giraffe? It's _____ .

3 _____ bus? It's _____ .

4 _____ _____

4 (2:53) Listen and number. Then write.

Where are the _____elephants_____ ?   _____

They're _____over the mountain_____   _____

_____ .   _____

_____   _____

_____   _____

5 Unscramble and write. Then match.

1 akle ___lake___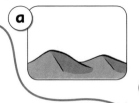

2 eas _____

3 slihl _____

4 staco _____

5 stap _____

6 rowdats _____

7 orthhug _____

8 donuar _____

6 Read and tick (✓).

1 They couldn't go towards the hills.

2 He could swim across the river.

3 She couldn't walk past the lake.

4 He could walk around the mountain.

7 (2:57) **Listen and number. Then write.**

Could she run past the lions?

_____ Yes, she could. _____

1

Could he swim through the lake?

_____

Could they go around hills?

_____

Could he walk towards the coast?

_____

8 (2:58) **Listen and write ✓ = could or ✗ = couldn't. Then write.**

1

✗

2

[ ]

3

[ ]

4

[ ]

1 We __couldn't__ go by bus but we ___could___ go by plane.

2 We _____ swim _____ the lake.

3 The huts were _____ the _____.

4 We couldn't go near the lions but we _____ walk _____ them.

9 **Write.** | climb play stay walk |

1 I ___walked___ in the rainforest yesterday.

2 We _____ in a hut last summer.

3 I _____ a tree last Saturday.

4 They _____ football at school last week.

10 Read the story again. Who's in a film? Write.

_____

11 Number the pictures in order.

12 Look at Activity 11 and write.

1 Who's wearing the costume?   It's _____Jenny_____.

2 Is Cleo on the building?   _____

3 Where's the wild cat?   It's _____ Ruby.

4 Where's the spider?   _____

5 Is the spider real?   _____

6 Is Sam scared?   _____

13 Choose a picture from Activity 11 and write.

> I like Picture d. The spider is funny.

I like Picture _____. _____

_____

14 **Read the words. Circle the pictures.**

circle   circus   ice   princess

15 (2:63) **Listen and connect the letters. Then write.**

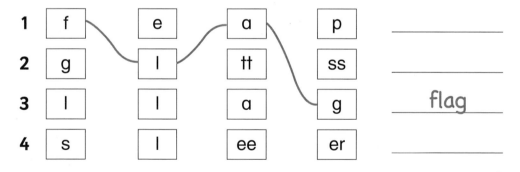

1 | f | e | a | p | _____
2 | g | l | tt | ss | _____
3 | l | l | a | g | _flag_
4 | s | l | ee | er | _____

16 (2:64) **Listen and write the words.**

1 _centre_   2 _____   3 _____   4 _____

17 (2:65) **Read aloud. Then listen and check.**

The princess is at home and the circus is here. It's a sunny day and the circus is funny but the princess isn't happy. She wants to go to the city.

18 **Read and write.**

| giant tarantula   hummingbird   parrot   tapir |

1 I've got a short neck.
I live near the river.
I eat bananas. What
animal am I?

___tapir___

2 I can fly. I've got a long
tail and colourful
feathers. What animal
am I?

_____

3 I can fly. I'm very small.
I like flowers. What
animal am I?

_____

4 I'm a big spider. I've got
long legs. I'm scary.
What animal am I?

_____

19 **Write about your favourite rainforest animal.**

My favourite rainforest animal is the piranha. Piranhas are
a kind of fish. They've got very sharp teeth. They live in the
Amazon River. They eat meat, fruit and seeds. I like them
because they're scary.

My favourite rainforest animal is the _____.

They've got _____.

They live _____.

They eat _____.

I like them because _____

_____.

Wider World

20 **Look and write.**

> playground   the Black Forest   tall trees and grass   the Irati Forest
> Spain   Germany

1

Forest: _____

Country: _____

Plants: _tall trees and grass_

2

Forest: _____

Country: _____

Place: _____

21 **Look at Activity 20 and write.**

1 This _____ Forest.

It's in _____.

There are _tall trees and grass_

there.

2 This _____ Forest.

It's in _____.

There's a _____ in

this forest.

Unit Review

22 Look and write.

Across ➡

1 The boat is moving towards the  .

3 I want to swim in the .

5 He wants to walk past the .

7 The monkeys are on the .

Down ⬇

2 A looks like a house.

4 A is taller than a hill.

6 A baby bird lives in a .

8 People use a to get from one side to the other.

23 (2:68) Listen and tick (✓).

About Me

24 Look and write.

1 <u>Where's the river?</u>

It's between the elephants
and the lions.

2 _____

They're near the hills.

3 Is the lake next to the river?

_____

4 Is the waterfall near the bridge?

_____

25 Imagine you were on the island in Activity 24. Write about what you could and couldn't do.

1 I could _____.

2 I couldn't _____.

26 Look and write. Then draw and write about you.

1 He _____ walked _____ through the forest yesterday.

2 She _____ last week.

3 I _____.

 I can talk about animals in different parts of the rainforest. ☐
I can talk about things in the past. ☐

7 Feelings

1 **Look and write.**

blushing   crying   frowning   laughing   shaking
shouting   smiling   yawning

①  He's ___laughing___ .

② She's _____ .

③ She's _____ .

④ He's _____ .

⑤  He's _____ .

⑥  He's _____ .

⑦  She's _____ .

⑧  She's _____ .

2 **Draw the correct faces.**

1 The police officer is angry.
   She's shouting.

2 The builder is tired.
   He's yawning.

3 The film star is sad.
   She's crying.

4 The firefighter is happy.
   He's smiling.

3 🔊 3:06 Listen and number.

4 Write.

1 he / shouting / angry

Why is he ___shouting___?

He's ___shouting___ because he's ___angry___.

2 you / yawning / tired

Why are you _____?

I'm _____ because I'm _____.

3 she / smiling / happy

_____

_____

4 he / shaking / ill

_____

_____

5 she / crying / hurt

_____

_____

6 he / frowning / bored

_____

_____

7 you / laughing / excited

_____

_____

5 Look and write.

| embarrassed | nervous | proud | relaxed | relieved | surprised | worried |

worried _____ _____

_____ _____ _____ _____

6 Look and write.

1 What's the matter?

I'm ___embarrassed___ .

2 How do you feel?

I feel _____ .

3 What's the matter?

4 How do you feel?

_____ _____

Lesson 3 vocabulary / grammar (talking about emotions)

7 🔊 3:10 **Listen and tick (✓).**

1 sad

a ✓   b ☐

2 nervous

a ☐   b ☐

3 worried

a ☐   b ☐

4 scared

a ☐   b ☐

8 **Look at Activity 7 and write.**

> being sick   crocodiles   flying   rainy days
> running   singing   snakes   swimming

1 What makes you feel sad? ___Rainy days___ make me feel ___sad___.

2 What makes _____?

_____ makes me feel _____.

3 What _____?

_____ makes _____.

4 _____?

_____ make _____.

9 **Match and write.**

1 He's worried.

2 I can't do this activity.

3 It's her birthday.

4 Get the books.

a Send _____ a present.

b Give ___him___ a hug.

c Put _____ on the shelf.

d Can you help _____?

10 Read the story again. What is 'PLEH'? Write.

_____

11 Look and write. Number the pictures in order.

> I feel scared now.   What's PLEH?   Have they got sharp claws?
> A film about Great Whites.   There's a diver!

a `1`

A film about
Great Whites.

b

_____

_____

c

_____

_____

d

_____

_____

e

_____

_____

12 Write about animals and how they make you feel.

1 I'm scared of _____ because _____.

2 I'm not scared of _____ because _____.

3 _____ make me feel happy because _____.

4 _____ make me feel worried because _____.

13 Find out more about one of the animals in Activity 12. Then write.

_____ live _____.

They're _____ metres long and have got _____

and _____. They eat _____.

14 Read the words. Circle the pictures.

page   gem   gentleman   large

ge   ge   **dge**

15 (3:15) Listen and connect the letters. Then write.

1	g	l	ee	n	*green*
2	c	r	ou	n	
3	t	p	oo	n	
4	s	r	ai	d	

16 (3:16) Listen and write the words.

1   *edge*   2 _____   3 _____   4 _____

17 (3:17) Read aloud. Then listen and check.

The gentleman looks at the gems. There are lots of small gems but he likes the large gem. 'How much is it?' he asks. Now he sighs, the price is too high.

18 (3:20) **Circle. Then listen to the music and number.**

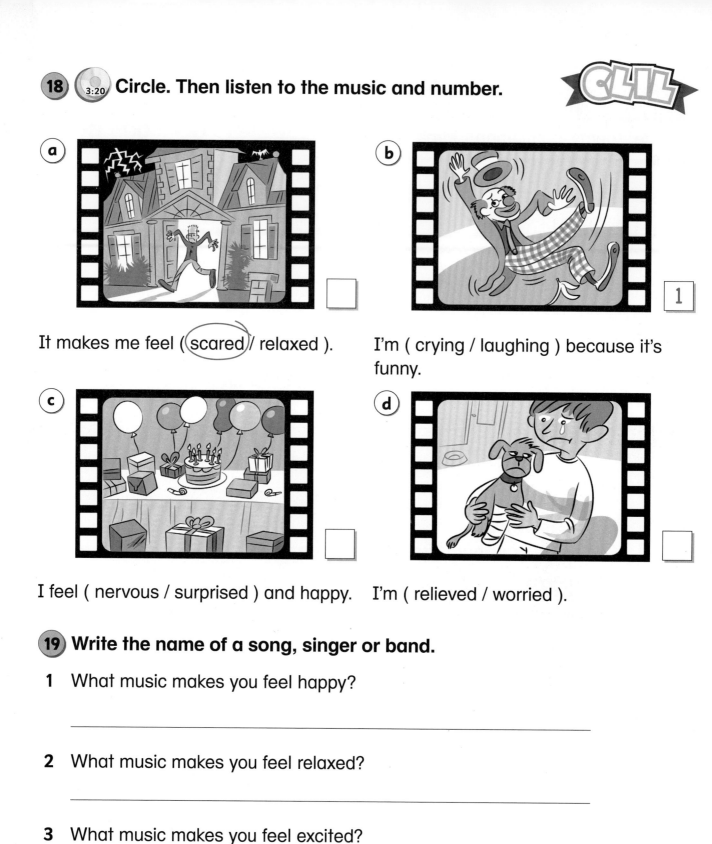

a It makes me feel (scared / relaxed).

b 1 I'm (crying / laughing) because it's funny.

c I feel (nervous / surprised) and happy.

d I'm (relieved / worried).

19 **Write the name of a song, singer or band.**

1 What music makes you feel happy?

_____

2 What music makes you feel relaxed?

_____

3 What music makes you feel excited?

_____

4 What music makes you feel sad?

_____

Wider World

20 Read and match.

1 Victoria's blog ✕

Hi! I'm Victoria. I go to a special music school. At school we have singing and dancing lessons every day. We go by bus and train to other schools and sing in concerts. Singing makes me feel happy because I love music.

Victoria, 10, South Africa

2 Mark's blog ✕

My name's Mark. I'm from Canada. Every year we have a festival called Winter Carnival. It makes me feel happy because it's fun. I go to Carnival with my family. We go skating, eat pancakes and drink hot chocolate. In the photo we're wearing beanies and scarves because it's cold.

Mark, 10, Canada

a

b

21 Read and write.

1 How does Victoria go to other schools?

She goes by bus and train.

2 Why does Victoria like singing?

_____

3 What makes Mark feel happy?

_____

4 What do they do at Winter Carnival?

_____

Unit Review

22 **Look and write.**

frowning	laughing	nervous	relaxed	relieved
	scared	shouting	smiling	

1

She's ____smiling____ because she's ____relieved____.

2

_____

_____

3 Aargh!

_____

_____

4 Ha-ha-ha!

_____

_____

23 **Write.**

angry	bored	happy	sad	nervous
	proud	hurt	tired	

crying	smiling	yawning	shaking
sad			

24 **Write.**

1 She likes flowers. Buy __her__ some for her birthday.

2 Can you help _____? They're worried about the test.

3 Can you make _____ lunch, please. We're hungry.

About Me

25 **Look and circle.**

My name's Mario. In this picture I'm ¹ (smiling / frowning) because I'm excited and ² (sad / happy). My ³ (football / basketball) team is this year's champion. Winning a game ⁴ (make / makes) me feel ⁵ (proud / embarrassed).

26 **Draw or stick a picture of yourself. Then write.**

My name's _____. In this picture I'm _____

_____

_____

_____

 I can talk about and give reasons for my feelings. ☐
I can ask others to share their feelings. ☐

1 **Match.**

fishing

horse-riding

kayaking

sailing

snorkelling

surfing

2 **Unscramble the words. Then look and write.**

farsorbud   file takecj   ginfshi ord   grinid stoob   norelsk   peldad

1 Ruby is _____fishing_____.
She's got a _____fishing rod_____.

2 John is wearing _____.
He's _____.

3 Jenny is _____ but she isn't wearing a _____.

4 Cleo is _____ but she hasn't got a _____.

5 Sam is on a _____. He's _____.

6 Madley Kool is wearing a _____. He's _____.

3 (3:28) **Listen, number and tick (✓).**

▢ a    b

▢ a    b

▢ a    b

1 a  ✓   b

4 **Write.**

1  ✓

Let's go horse-riding!

Great idea! I love ___horse-riding___ .

2  ✗

_____!

Sorry, I don't like _____ .

3  ✗

_____

_____

4  ✓

_____

_____

Have you got _____?

Yes, I have.

5 **Look and write.**

> bungee jumping   scuba diving   hang gliding   rafting   rock climbing

hang gliding   _____   _____

_____   _____

6 **Write. Then listen and match.**

> bored with   crazy about   fond of   scared of   terrified of

(1)   crazy about

(2)   _____

(3)   _____

(4)   _____

(5)   _____

7 Look at Activity 6 and write.

1 What's she ___crazy about___ ? She's _crazy about scuba diving_ .

2 What's _____? _____

3 _____ _____

4 _____ _____

5 _____ _____

8 Look and write.

1 What are you going to do? ___I'm going to go sailing.___

2 _____ they _____? _____

3 _____ she _____? _____

9 Write about yourself. Then draw or stick a picture.

What are you terrified of? I'm terrified of _____ _____.	What are you going to do tomorrow? I'm _____ _____.

10 Read the story again. How does Cleo help Madley Kool? Write.

_____

11 Number the pictures in order.

12 Look and write.

acting   good   making   film star   scared of   sharks

Madley Kool is a great ¹_____film star_____. He's

crazy about ²_____ adventure films.

His new film is _Great White Sharks_. In this

film there are some big ³_____.

Madley Kool is ⁴_____ sharks but he's

a ⁵_____ actor. He says, 'Sharks are

scary but I like ⁶_____.'

13 Write.

1 What's Madley Kool crazy about? _____

_____

2 What's he scared of? _____

14 **Read the words. Circle the pictures.**

dolphin   phone   whale   whisper

15 (3:37) **Listen and connect the letters. Then write.**

1	p	i	n	y	_____
2	b	u	nn	p	_____
3	t	u	m	le	_____
4	f	ai	ck	t	_paint_

16 (3:38) **Listen and write the words.**

1   _elephant_   2   _____   3   _____   4   _____

17 (3:39) **Read aloud. Then listen and check.**

Look, the whale and the dolphin are on the phone! Here comes the shark.
The fish are whispering. What's that on his head? Oh, it's a funny hat!

18 **Write.**

colourful fish hot rainforests sea sea animals white

1   Coral reefs are called the _____ rainforests _____ of the sea.

2   There are a lot of _____ and _____ on coral reefs.

3   Coral reefs are _____.

4   Some coral reefs die when the _____ becomes too

    _____.

5   Dead coral reefs are _____ in colour.

19 **Write.**

butterfly   butterfly fish   seahorse   lion   parrot parrot fish   sea snake   horse   snake   starfish

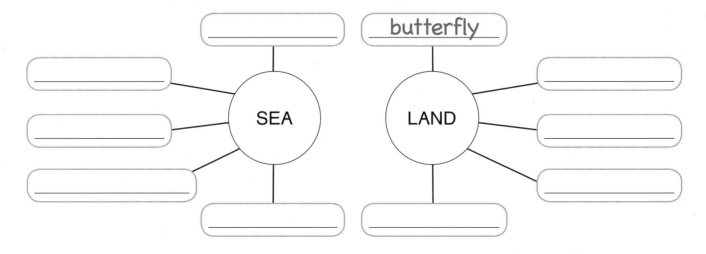

SEA

_____ butterfly

LAND

20 **Write.**

Why are most coral reefs found in warm seas?

_____

Wider World

21 Look and write.

rafting   horse-riding   beach volleyball   kayaking   surfing   snorkelling

1

horse-riding

2

_____

3

_____

4

_____

5

_____

6

_____

22 Plan a summer camp. Then write.

Monday	Tuesday	Wednesday
go rafting		

1 On Monday we're going to _go rafting_ , _____ and _____.

2 On Tuesday _____.

3 _____

Lesson 8 wider world (summer camps)

85

Unit Review

23 **Look and write.**

1 **A:** Let's go ___sailing___ ! Have you got
a ___life jacket___ ?

B: No, ___I haven't___ .

2 **A:** _____

Have _____ ?

B: Yes, _____ .

3 **A:** _____

B: Great idea. I love _____ .

I like watching the fish.

4 **A:** _____

B: Sorry, _____

_____ . I'm scared of it.

5 **A:** What are you going to do next week?

B: I'm _____

_____ .

6 **A:** What are _____ ?

B: I'm _____

_____ .

About Me

24 **Look and write.**

Hi, Gerry,

I'm having a great time here. In the morning I go

¹ _____horse-riding_____. I'm fond of it. It makes me feel relaxed. In the

evening we go ² _____. But I'm

³ _____ it. I don't like it very much. We're

going to go ⁴ _____ on Saturday. I'm

⁵ _____ it. It makes me feel proud that I can do it.

Tomorrow I'm going to go ⁶ _____.

Raphael

25 **Pretend you are on holiday. Write an email to a friend.**

○○○ [_____]

_____

_____

_____

_____

_____

_____

I can make, accept and refuse invitations. ☐

I can talk about what I'm going to do in the future. ☐

1 Look and write.

1 What's his name? _____

2 What _____?

He likes making films.

3 Why _____?

He's smiling because he's happy.

2 🎵 3:44 Listen and circle.

	a	b	c
1	a) eating with Madley Kool	b) meeting Madley Kool	c) looking for Madley Kool
2	a) boys	b) girls	c) cats
3	a)	b)	c)
4	a)	b)	c)
5	a)	b)	c)
6	a)	b)	c)
7	a) relaxed	b) worried	c) proud
8	a) three	b) four	c) five

3 Write.

1

Who's your favourite character in the story?

My favourite character is _____
_____ .

2

What's your favourite chant about?

My favourite chant is about _____
_____ .

3

What's your favourite song about?

_____
_____

4 Think of your favourite film star. Stick a picture of him/her in a scene from a film. Then write.

My favourite film star is _____ .

This scene is from the film _____ .

In this scene he/she is _____ . I like this scene because

it makes me feel _____ .

5 (3:45) **Listen and read about Willie. Then write about yourself.**

My name is Willie. I'm 10 years old. I like playing the guitar and surfing the Internet in my free time. I don't like painting or drawing. My favourite wild animal is the gorilla. Gorillas live in the rainforest and they eat leaves and fruit.

My name is _____

_____

_____

6 **Look and write.**

Nov. 4, Sun.	Nov. 5, Mon.	Nov. 6, Tues.	Nov. 7, Wed.	Nov. 8, Thurs.	Nov. 9, Fri.	Nov. 10, Sat.
24°C	19°C	20°C	25°C	20°C	19°C	19°C

1 It's Tuesday. What's the weather like today?   It's _____wet_____.

2 It's Sunday. What's the temperature today?   It's _____.

3 It's Thursday. Is it humid?   _____, it _____.

4 It's Saturday. What's the weather like today?   There's _____

_____.

5 It's Wednesday. Is it stormy?   _____

6 It's Monday. Is it wet?   _____

7 (3:46) **Listen and read about Judy. Then write about yourself.**

My name is Judy. I'm 11 years old. I study hard every day. I play basketball with my friends on Wednesdays. I learn to cook with my grandmother on Saturdays. When I grow up I want to be a lawyer or a journalist.

My name is _____

_____

_____

_____

8 (3:47) **Listen and write.**

1 What makes Amy feel ...

   a proud? ____playing the piano____

   b nervous? _____

2 What's Amy ...

   a fond of? _____

   b bored with? _____

9 **Write.**

1 What's a way of talking that is not the telephone? ____chatting online____

2 What animal lives in rivers and only eats meat? _____

3 What weather has thunder and lightning? _____

4 What time is between morning and afternoon? _____

5 What do you call a person who takes photos? _____

6 What do you call the place where baby birds live? _____

7 How do people feel if they do well at something? _____

8 What do you need to go kayaking? _____

1 Find, circle and write the Halloween words.

1   _____moon_____

2   _____

3   _____

4   _____

5   _____

n	o	s	s	m	y	s	e	s	s
m	l	n	s	o	r	l	o	s	m
m	e	m	e	e	m	e	l	n	m
t	a	o	n	f	w	n	o	n	k
y	s	n	e	e	e	n	m	e	e
s	n	s	t	r	l	l	o	e	n
m	o	t	o	o	w	r	o	w	l
s	k	e	l	e	t	o	n	o	o
t	o	r	t	o	o	n	l	r	o
w	o	l	b	o	n	e	n	n	s

2 Look and write.

1 The children have got

   bags of ____sweets____ .

2 There are _____ owls.

3 The _____

   has got many bones.

4 The witch is on a

   _____ .

5 The children are ghosts

   and _____ .

Christmas Day

1 Find, circle and write the Christmas words.

1. _____lunch_____
2. _____
3. _____
4. _____
5. _____
6. _____
7. _____

n	e	l	p	l	i	l	p	r	l
s	c	r	a	c	k	e	r	n	g
s	l	b	h	e	h	n	e	m	s
n	l	u	n	c	h	p	s	l	n
o	r	s	p	i	c	t	e	i	o
w	n	p	u	d	d	i	n	g	w
m	p	r	e	s	e	n	t	h	b
a	p	w	h	r	n	t	r	t	a
n	r	k	n	r	c	n	h	s	l
n	c	t	k	l	i	w	g	u	l

2 Write.

> songs   presents   lights   snowman   turkey   pudding   snowballs

At Christmas we decorate a Christmas tree with [1]_____lights_____.

We open and play with our [2]_____. Then we cook a

lunch with [3]_____ and Christmas [4]_____.

When it's snowy we play with [5]_____ and make a

[6]_____. In the evening we sing Christmas [7]_____.

1 Find, circle and write the Easter words.

1 _jelly beans_

2 _____

3 _____

4 _____

5 _____

6 _____

c	c	t	e	n	e	o	o	b	r
l	h	s	m	e	g	g	s	a	o
o	o	c	s	c	t	a	n	s	t
l	c	e	h	o	g	s	s	k	k
t	o	t	b	b	e	c	c	e	o
a	l	r	n	u	i	a	n	t	a
b	a	a	s	n	e	t	a	b	l
g	t	i	e	n	l	m	b	y	j
j	e	l	l	y	b	e	a	n	s
c	l	j	t	o	l	t	e	h	k

2 Look, match and write.

> chocolate   eating   flowers   trail

①

②

③

④

a The girl has got _____ eggs.

b Mum has got a basket of _____.

c The boy is _____ a chocolate bunny.

d Peter Cottontail is hopping down a _trail_.

Mother's Day

1 **Match.**

toast

tea

box of chocolates

rose

Mum

present

2 **Read. Then write your own note and draw a picture.**

Dear Mum,
Happy Mother's Day!
You are my best friend.
I love you,
John

Review

Welcome and Unit 1

1 Answer the questions.

1 What's your name? _____

2 How old are you? _____

3 How old is your friend? _____

4 Is your friend older than you? _____

5 What's his/her favourite colour? _____

2 Complete the sentences.

1 Peter is ___taller than___ (tall) Cindy.

2 The cat is _____ (small) the dog.

3 My hands are _____ (big) my sister's hands.

4 Kim is _____ (young) Paul.

5 My dad is _____ (old) me.

3 Write sentences about yourself.

| skiing   cooking   watching TV   playing the guitar   playing computer games |

I like ...   I don't like ...

1 _____   1 _____

2 _____   2 _____

3 _____   3 _____

4 Ask a partner the questions. Then write the answers.

1 What do you like doing? _____

2 Do you like skiing? _____

3 What does your mum like doing? _____

4 Does she like reading the newspaper? _____

Unit 2

1 **Find 8 animals and write.**

i	o	c	o	m	l	o	g	z
n	h	h	c	o	l	n	o	r
n	e	i	f	z	e	b	r	a
h	l	p	a	n	d	a	i	l
e	r	p	c	a	m	e	l	f
c	r	o	c	o	d	i	l	e
l	i	o	n	n	a	z	a	z
f	h	l	g	o	y	m	a	m
e	l	e	p	h	a	n	t	r

1 _gorilla_   2 _____

3 _____ 4 _____

5 _____ 6 _____

7 _____ 8 _____

2 **Write about the animals.**

> forests   grass   rivers   meat   leaves   deserts

1 Zebras eat _____grass_____.   2 Hippos live in _____.

3 Giraffes eat _____.   4 Camels live in _____.

5 Lions eat _____.   6 Pandas live in _____.

3 **Answer the questions.**

1 Do lions eat leaves?   _No, they don't._____

2 Do monkeys eat fruit?   _____

3 Where do gorillas live?   _____

4 Where do elephants live?   _____

5 What do gorillas eat?   _____

4 **Match.**

1 Crocodiles can swim   **a** fast.

2 Crocodiles can't run   **b** a lot of teeth.

3 Crocodiles have got   **c** in rivers.

4 Crocodiles eat   **d** meat and fish.

5 Crocodiles live   **e** very well.

Unit 3

1 **Answer the questions.**

1 What's the weather like today? _____

2 What's the temperature today? _____

3 Is it warm? _____

4 Is it stormy? _____

2 **Write about what you and your partner do in each season.**

1 In spring …
I _____ . He/She _____ .

2 In summer …
I _____ . He/She _____ .

3 In autumn …
I _____ . He/She _____ .

4 In winter …
I _____ . He/She _____ .

3 **Draw and write about the weather.**

yesterday

last winter

1 _____   2 _____

4 **Write about your favourite season.**

My favourite season is _____ . The weather is _____

and _____ . In _____ I like _____ .

Unit 4

1 **Write *do* or *have*.**

1 ____have____ music lessons

2 _____ karate

3 _____ gymnastics

4 _____ ballet lessons

2 **Write *practise* or *learn to*.**

1 ____practise____ the violin

2 _____ draw

3 _____ cook

4 _____ the piano

3 **Write about your week.**

1 What do you do on Mondays? _____

2 What do you do on Fridays? _____

3 What do you do on Saturdays? _____

4 When do you study English? _____

5 When do you study Maths? _____

4 **Ask your partner about his/her week. Then write the answers.**

1 What does he/she do on Mondays? _____

2 What does he/she do on Fridays? _____

3 What does he/she do on Saturdays? _____

4 When does he/she study English? _____

5 When does he/she study Maths? _____

5 **Write about yourself.**   always   often   never

1 _____

2 _____

3 _____

Unit 5

1 Write the words in alphabetical order.

singer journalist mechanic lawyer firefighter
builder carpenter photographer astronaut

1 _____astronaut_____ 2 _____ 3 _____

4 _____ 5 _____ 6 _____

7 _____ 8 _____ 9 _____

2 Write about what you and your partner want to and don't want to be.

want to be

1 I _____ because _____.

2 He/She _____ because _____.

don't want to be

1 I _____.

2 He/She_____.

3 Write.

1 Do you want to be a farmer?_____No, I don't._____ (✗)

2 Does he want to be a journalist? _____ (✓)

3 What does she want to be? _____ (model)

4 _____ No, I don't want to be an athlete.

5 _____ He wants to be a lawyer.

4 Draw and write about your dream job.

I want to be _____

because _____

_____.

Unit 6

l	g	i	o	t	c	r	e	r
o	l	b	v	n	s	b	e	l
e	c	r	i	v	e	r	u	h
m	o	u	n	t	a	i	n	i
l	a	k	e	r	p	d	a	l
n	s	s	i	l	s	g	v	l
s	t	i	n	h	m	t	n	n
o	l	i	d	i	t	s	r	n
e	h	u	t	o	s	t	u	u

1 Find 8 nature words and write.

1 _river_ 2 _____
3 _____ 4 _____
5 _____ 6 _____
7 _____ 8 _____

2 Read and draw.

1 The river is between the hut and the mountain.
2 The monkey is near the hut.
3 The crocodile is in the river.
4 The birds are over the mountain.

3 Describe what you *could* and *couldn't* do.

| walk   swim   watch   run   see   climb |

I could …   I couldn't …

1 _____   1 _____

2 _____   2 _____

4 Write.

1 He ___hiked___ (hike) through the mountains yesterday.

2 She _____ (climb) a tree in the rainforest last summer.

3 I _____ (watch) the gorillas last week.

4 They _____ (walk) to school last Monday.

Unit 7

1 **Write the words in alphabetical order.**

crying shouting yawning frowning laughing blushing smiling shaking drinking

1 _____blushing_____   2 _____   3 _____

4 _____   5 _____   6 _____

7 _____   8 _____   9 _____

2 **Write.**

angry crying smiling nervous blushing feel

1 He's _____smiling_____ because he's relaxed.

2 Tests make her _____.

3 I'm _____ because I'm sad.

4 My friend is _____ because he's embarrassed.

5 I'm shouting because I'm _____.

6 How do you feel? I _____ relieved.

3 **Write the questions.**

1 _Why are you crying_____? I'm crying because I'm sad.

2 _____? She's nervous because she has a test.

3 _____? He's shouting because he's angry.

4 _____? I'm embarrassed.

5 _____? I feel happy.

4 **Answer about yourself.**

1 What makes you feel nervous? _____

2 What makes you feel proud? _____

3 What makes you feel relaxed? _____

4 What makes you feel worried? _____

Unit 8

1 Write the words in alphabetical order.

scuba diving   snorkelling   hang gliding   kayaking   fishing
bungee jumping   rafting   horse-riding   rock climbing

1 _bungee jumping_   2 _____   3 _____
4 _____   5 _____   6 _____
7 _____   8 _____   9 _____

2 Write.

1

A: Let's go snorkelling.

B: Great idea. I _love snorkelling_.

3

A: Have you got riding boots?

B: No, _____.

2

A: _____

B: Sorry, I don't like hang gliding.

4

A: _____

B: Yes, I have. I've got a fishing rod.

3 Answer about yourself.

1 What are you scared of? _____

2 What are you fond of? _____

3 What are you bored with? _____

4 What are you terrified of? _____

5 What are you crazy about? _____

4 Answer about yourself.

1 What are you going to do tomorrow morning? _____

_____

2 What are you going to do next week? _____

_____

3 What are you going to do next summer? _____

_____

Picture dictionary

Unit 1

Leisure activities

skiing

cooking

watching TV

playing the guitar

playing computer games

skateboarding

reading the newspaper

chatting online

skipping

painting

playing hockey

reading magazines

watching films

surfing the Internet

walking the dog

riding a scooter

Special houses

lighthouse

stairs

Unit 2
Wild animals/Food/Habitats

giraffe   elephant   lion   monkey   hippo   crocodile

leaves   grass   fruit   meat   crab   camel

zebra   panda   gorilla   river   desert   grassland

forest   rainforest   herbivore   carnivore   omnivore   grasshopper

mouse   snake   eagle   orangutan   lion cub

Unit 3
Weather

warm

humid

wet

stormy

lightning

thunder

temperature

degrees

Seasonal activities

go camping

go water skiing

go hiking

go snowboarding

Seasons

spring

summer

autumn

winter

Natural disasters

hurricane

wave

earthquake

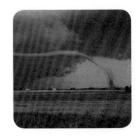
tornado

Unit 4
Activities

have music lessons

have ballet lessons

do karate

do gymnastics

practise the piano

practise the violin

learn to draw

learn to cook

study English

study Maths

Time

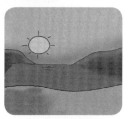
morning

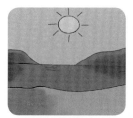
midday

afternoon

evening

2.15   a quarter past 2

2.30
half past 2

2.45
a quarter to 3

Going to school

road

radio

plane

snowmobile

Unit 5
Jobs

builder

firefighter

police officer

basketball player

film star

ballet dancer

astronaut

singer

model

journalist

photographer

carpenter

mechanic

lawyer

athlete

Future jobs

champion

Olympic Games

coach

train

Unit 6
Nature

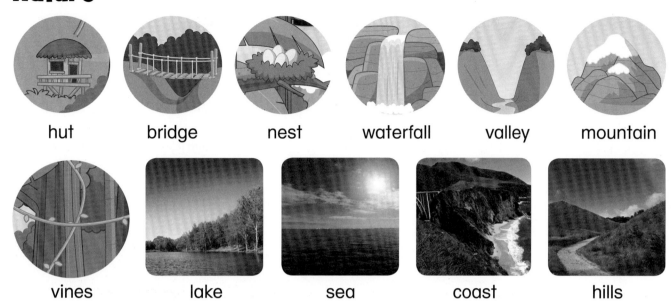

hut   bridge   nest   waterfall   valley   mountain

vines   lake   sea   coast   hills

Prepositions

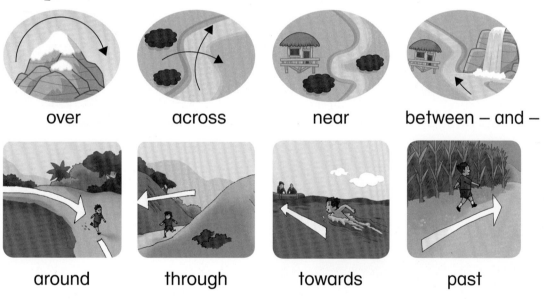

over   across   near   between – and –

around   through   towards   past

Rainforest

parrot   hummingbird   nectar   tapir   giant tarantula

Unit 7
Actions/Emotions

crying	shouting	yawning	frowning	laughing
blushing	smiling	shaking	nervous	proud
relieved	surprised	relaxed	embarrassed	worried

Cultural traditions

dragon dance	lantern	traditional dress